Proverbs for Living a Lovely Life

THE Wisdom of GRACE

DIANE ROBLIN-LEE

Library and Archives Canada Cataloguing in Publication

Roblin-Lee, Diane, 1945-
     The wisdom of Grace / Diane Roblin-Lee.

Includes index.
ISBN 978-1-896213-45-3

     1. Wisdom--Quotations, maxims, etc. 2. Conduct of life--Quotations, maxims, etc. 3. Roblin, Grace. I. Title.

BJ1581.2.R623 2009   158.1   C2008-907610-9

© 2009 Diane Roblin-Lee

PUBLISHED IN CANADA
byDesign Media
www.bydesignmedia.ca

COVER & INTERIOR DESIGN — Diane Roblin-Lee

All rights reserved. No part of this publication may be reproduced, stored in a retrieval system, or transmitted in any form or by any means without prior permission of the copyright owner.

This little book is dedicated
to you who read it,
in the hopes that sharing
the essence of my mother,
Ella Mariah Grace (Irwin) Roblin,
will reaffirm priceless values,
help smooth the path ahead,
and bring blessing to your life
as she always did, so abundantly, to mine.

Diane Roblin-Lee

Prologue

Progress doesn't always mean leaving the past behind and venturing forth into uncharted realms. Sometimes it means trying new things, finding they don't work and then reaffirming whatever worked.

It takes the reading of only one newspaper to recognize that much of the "progress" we've made isn't progress at all.

It's time to look back and rediscover the foundations of society that existed before the advent of our fifty percent divorce rate and the disintegration of family structures.

The nuggets of wisdom contained herein may be distasteful to modern thinkers who decry a life lived in humility and service to others.

But who can argue with results?

Grace Roblin celebrated her 60th wedding anniversary, a rarity today. Through many ups and downs, she and her husband, a Baptist minister, found a depth of love and commitment that can come only through many years of shared lives.

Grace was content with her circumstances. Rather than demanding her rights, her own time and her own space, she served God, her husband, children and community, in that order. Blessing everyone she touched along the way, she was surrounded by love, respect and admiration.

The results of Grace's life are the results everyone wants from life. The problem is that in this modern society, we don't like the way she got them. We would have told her she needed to find herself, to be more independent, to look after number one.

But it's our modern philosophy that landed us where we are. Perhaps it's time to reaffirm the wisdom we've discarded and the way of life that worked. There's no mystery about where Grace got her wisdom. It's just practical Christianity—life lived God's way.

Ella Mariah Grace (Irwin) Roblin

1908-2005

Known to all as "Grace," with unusual wisdom
and natural elegance, she was aptly named.

Foreword

Diane Roblin-Lee's clarity in expressing profound concepts never fails to leave me with the thought, "I wish I could've said it like that."

I knew and highly respected Diane's mother and father, Reverend Al and Grace Roblin. My reaction to memories of them produce in me the question in the form of a prayer, "O Lord, would you bless us by giving us more role models of such grace, intelligence, compassion and dedication to Christ?"

In *The Wisdom of Grace,* Diane is generously giving all of us a treasure, a gift of present and eternal values through the wonderful example of her precious mother, Grace.

David Mainse
Founder - *100 Huntley Street*
Crossroads Christian Communications Inc.

The Life of Grace — 207

Topics

Aging — *179, 193, 195*
Accomplishments — *81, 105, 145, 151, 157, 161*
Bossiness — *49*
Choices — *37, 63, 151*
Circumstances — *11, 25, 31, 155, 157, 171, 187*
Communication — *13, 27, 39, 41, 109*
Confidence — *43*
Consequences — *31, 151*
Controlling spirit — *75*
Daily life — *105, 119, 129, 131, 133, 139 157, 165.*
167, 189, 197
Divorce — *107, 109*
Emotions — *83, 141, 143, 147*
Endurance — *93*
Eternity — *151, 159, 161, 189, 191*
197, 203
Faith — *127, 153, 155, 169, 171*
Family — *19, 21, 89, 99*
Flaws — *35*
Forgiveness — *15*
Fulfillment — *59, 135, 151, 159, 183, 193*
Future — *85, 151, 193*

Fresh start	29
Friendship	61, 79, 174
Gentility	55
Happiness	51, 59, 95, 167, 177, 183
Health	103
Literature	53
Love	65, 67
Marriage	71, 73, 77, 107, 173, 174, 175, 177, 181
Offense	37, 47
Parenting	91, 97, 121, 125, 137, 205
Prayer	101, 169, 171, 187, 195, 199
Relationships	67
Relaxing	45
Self-esteem	43
Sin	185
Sorrow	33, 57
Spiritual growth	17, 87, 115, 117, 123, 131, 149, 153, 183, 203
Stepping out	145
Testing	69, 173
Will	11
Wisdom	23, 113, 151, 163
Youth	65, 131, 179

We have no control over the
circumstances into which we are born.
Some are born poor, some rich,
some plain, some gifted.

There are two things we are
given equally—time and will.
It's how we use these gifts that determines
the eventual value of our lives.

Welcomed words that soak
into a warm spot in one's heart
are whispered — not yelled.

Forgive and become like Jesus,
or don't forgive and become
like the person you're not forgiving.

Spiritual growth is more a matter of
abiding than trying to grow.

Growing comes by submitting to,
and moving with, a life-force.
All the trying in the world
cannot make a doll grow, but a living
baby stretches and grows
with no effort on its part.
It has the force of life within.

Spiritual growth depends on the presence of the
life-force of the Holy Spirit. Once filled with Him,
one cannot help but grow.

While an earthly family may last a lifetime, a spiritual family lasts for eternity.

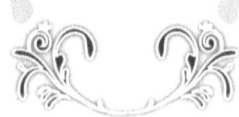

The extended family was designed by God as a
ready-made support group for the mutual
encouragement of the
developing generations.

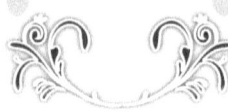

It's a wise person who lives life thinking about what makes God happy – instead of what makes oneself happy.

An extremity of circumstances
is God's opportunity
to prove Himself faithful.

If you don't have something good to say about
someone, it's best to be quiet.

We don't know what motivates people
to do the things they do.
We just have to bear with them
and understand that
people have to live out their own lives.

*E*ach morning
turns the page on a new day.

Sharing breakfast with
the household strengthens unity.
It fortifies everyone for dealing
with the carryover from
yesterday and the challenges
today will bring.

Food for the body becomes nourishment for the
heart when enjoyed in an atmosphere of pleasant
conversation and noisy love.

There are those who can't seem to learn from
anything but their own mistakes.

Where the misdirected actions of others
affect our own lives, we have to quietly shift gears,
alter our plans, forgive, love and
patiently wait for God to bring good
out of the circumstances.

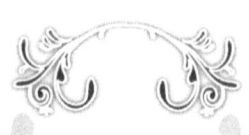

When some great sorrow,
like a tsunami wave,
roars over your heart with peace-destroying power,
hold fast to the reality
that this, too, shall pass.

*"Weeping may endure for a night,
but joy comes in the morning."*

Psalm 30:5

It's easy to recognize the faults of others,
but fixing one's own is the work of a lifetime.

Oddly, the things we most dislike about
others are the things we fear
may reside in us.

Taking personal offense from the words or
actions of others is like eating poison
offered from their hands.

Sluff the hurt away
with a kind thought or word.

Choose to live a lovely life.

To the discerning listener, one who speaks badly
of others is the one who looks small.

Feeding a relationship with unkind words
about another is like drinking
poisoned tea together.

Kind words endear a speaker to a listener.

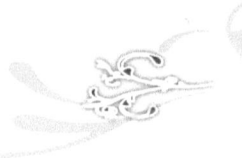

Communication can be overrated.
Once words leave the mouth,
they can never be retrieved.

To express negative feelings that have not yet
been taken to the Lord for His working,
is to expose the mess Satan is trying to make in
one's life as though it were an accomplished feat.

*W*e have made a god out of *self*-esteem in this century.

But God says we need to esteem *others* higher than *ourselves*.

On the other hand, don't we *need* *self*-esteem to have the confidence to face the challenges of life?

Confidence based on our own abilities or possessions has a weak foundation. We need Christ-confidence—confidence built on the promise that we can do *"all things through Christ who strengthens us."*
*P*hilippians 4:13

The higher we esteem Christ, the more confidence we have to step out, mindful of living our lives through His power.

Ahhhh the joy of relaxation when the mind is
cleared by finished chores
and completed tasks.

1928 Chevrolet

Kill a grudge the moment you recognize it.
Get rid of it as you would
a rat in your pantry.

$\mathcal{B}$ossiness in women
is most unattractive.
We can do better.

No one on this planet can possibly be
a constant source of happiness for another.
Disappointment in human relationships is part
of the raw material God allows to
strengthen and mature us.

The sooner we learn that happiness comes from giving it to another, the less we'll be tested
in our relationships.

What a pleasure to
share good literature!

While television isolates families and friends from
one another, a good book read aloud gives
mutual pleasure, intertwining the
thoughts and hearts of the readers.

True gentility blossoms from a quietly patient spirit; one that makes allowances for the faults in others and calls on love to cover the inevitable disappointments of life.

No life is untouched by sorrow.
We choose to live either
as victims or as overcomers.
Imposing one's complaints on
another doubles the burden.

How much better to wrap up our wounded hearts
and shattered dreams,
ask Jesus to take the package away,
look around and see how we can
lessen the burden of another.

Fulfillment comes not by running away from
one's responsibilities to explore the grass
on the other side of the fence.

Fulfillment is found when one asks God to reveal
His purpose for his or her life,
then finds a need and uses God-given
abilities to help satisfy it.

A soul will be blessed by a gentle, understanding friend far more than by one who comes prepared to take control and make demands.

No matter what anyone may do to another, no one can take away one's choice of how to respond to the offense.

Young lovers, like fragrant roses,
eventually grow old, wither and die.
It's how they nurture their love in the bloom of
youth that determines the longevity
of its sweet fragrance.

There's no such thing as "falling" in or out of
love. One decides whether or not to
make advances or respond to another.

Once the mind says, "yes," one allows
his or her emotions to intertwine
with those of the other.

Taking time to assess the wisdom of a
relationship, before allowing emotions
to cloud judgement, results in greater
likelihood of lining oneself up
with God's perfect plan.

 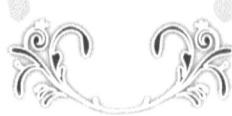 

Rev. Alva Stewart Roblin

We are all tested every day, in every way.

Whether we pass or fail depends on
the motivation of our hearts,
our diligence
and our sensitivity to ministering
to the needs of others.

If people were aware beforehand,
of the challenges that follow marriage,
there might be far fewer weddings!
People would doubt they would have the ability
to face the trials.

But God gives grace when it is needed.
He is our ever-present strength in
times of trouble and can carry us
through whatever may come.

In the final accounting, marriage has little to do
with the actions of a spouse. Marriage is
one place in life where it
really is "all about me."

Marriage is about how we allow God to refine us in
the midst of our circumstances and how we
help our partners to grow.

When we step out of marriage (except in the case
of adultery or physical abuse), we step out
of a priceless finishing school.

When we focus on being the individual
God wants us to be,
He fixes the circumstances.

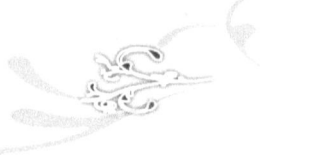

*1933 Wedding Cake
Iced by Grace's new husband!*

Allowing others to try their hand at something
we might prefer to control, opens the door to a
sharing of experience, the opportunity for
giving of encouragement and
the making of a memory.

Demanding control not only closes those doors, but
plants seeds of discouragement,
defeat and isolation.

𝓕eeling like an outsider in the family of one's
spouse is natural, because it's not
the family of birth.

One's job is to make happy memories with in-laws
that will progressively bind all together
as a new family
with a joint future in which
children have the security to grow.

While there are growing pains in every family, God
will bring beauty if one presses through troubles
with love and selflessness.

*I*ntimate chats with dear friends are
opportunities to share God's grace
and salt another's trials with His promises.

It's the pure intent of a deed done that is to be
treasured—not the applause that may
thunder at its heels which many
seek after as fame.

Feelings are not reliable.
God's promises must be the engine
that drives our lives—
our emotions the caboose.

No matter how we feel, if we are faithful and do
what we know to be right,
our lives will stay on track
and good feelings will follow.

Who can know what the future holds?

Taking the journey of life is like
walking through a lovely forest at night,
surrounded by great beauty and unknown dangers.

God holds the flashlight,
giving only enough light for the next footstep.

Faith in His ability to conquer any terrors ahead
drives fear from our paths.

The maturity of one's spirituality is measured by the time gap between sin and repentance.

When parents bring a baby into the world,
they enter into a sacred trust
with all those who surround the baby—
the grandparents, aunts, uncles and cousins.

All those whom God has organized into a family
group to love and support the child,
trust the parents to have the maturity,
stability and sensitivity not to break
the hearts they open to receive the child.

When a parent opts for divorce and
ruthlessly rips the bonds that tie a child to his or
her extended family, waves of heartbreak swell
from the epicenter—often unrecognized by
the preoccupied perpetrator.

We have to do whatever it takes to protect and
cherish the precious hearts around us.

The four greatest gifts a loving parent can lavish
upon a child are love, wisdom,
discipline and understanding.

The secret of endurance is to be still
and know that God is working.

Happiness comes by developing
the responses God wants us to have
to the circumstances
He has allowed around us.

"The fruit of the Spirit is love, joy, peace, patience,
kindness, goodness, faithfulness,
gentleness and self-control."

Galatians 5:22

Children are not possessions.
They are unique individuals entrusted by God
to our care and guidance.

They need to be raised with the same
kindness, dignity, attention and focus
one would give to the child of a president
—because—
they are children of the King of kings!

We flatter those we barely know
and rush to please our guests.

We need to tend with greatest care
those we love, who will, we hope,
share our lives forever.

𝒫rayer is a daily discipline.
Sometimes it feels unfruitful—but that's just from
our perspective. God wouldn't have taught
us to pray if it had no purpose.

If we don't take time to hear God's voice,
the products of our lives will be much
less substantial than they might be.

𝓑alance and moderation are the keys
to healthy living, body, soul and spirit.
All work and no fun makes one dull indeed.

Here and there, along life's way, there may be
honors, awards and recognition for a job well done.
But mostly, life is just a matter of putting one foot
after the other, moment by moment,
doing what needs to be done.

In between performing His miracles,
Jesus washed the feet of His disciples.

We wash the feet of those around us
as we tend to their needs, listen to their hearts
and encourage them on to do their best.

Yes, marriage can be painful at times—
but so is childbirth.
Giving up before the deep companionship
of mature marriage is forged,
is like aborting a beautiful child.

𝒥ust as God spoke His world into existence, we speak our worlds into existence by the things we say to those around us.

𝒟ivorce masquerades
as an exit from problems.

In reality, it is an entrance—
an entrance into a whole new set
of problems, often more complicated
and frustrating than the first set.

Satan's purpose is to destroy people.
His arena is most often the family.
Once unmasked and confronted
by the Name of Jesus, he has to flee.

If one has tried one's best but the spouse is
unwilling, all is not lost.
Nothing comes as a surprise to God.
Tenderly, He will take a broken heart and turn its
lessons into great treasure as He restores hope to
the hopeless, brings healing to bruised hearts and
unfolds His vision for the wonderful life ahead.

People say, "I believe this or that," implying that their minds can conceive of things superior to what God says.

Whatever does not line up with God's plumb-line is foolishness and vanity.

Supposing oneself to have wisdom superior to that of one's Creator is the ultimate in arrogance.

God loves you too much
to let you stay the way you are.

If you want to lift people up,
you have to be on higher ground.

Although our work may at times seem unimportant, if we do it in a manner we know would be
pleasing to God—
unpretentiously,
without any thought of distinction—
it can become outstanding as
He weaves it into His great plan.

The very word, 'mothers'
is almost all about 'others.'

Character and skill are the results
of habits developed
through faithful repetition.

Even the tortoise reached the ark,
one step at a time.

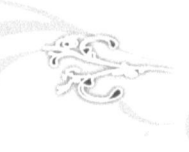

Teaching obedience to children prepares them
to be obedient to God in later life.

Parents who do not teach their children to obey,
do them no favors.

We serve the same God who
rescued Moses from the bulrushes,
parted the Red Sea and
made the lame man walk.

Nothing is too hard for Him.

The promise of one's future is
in one's daily routine.

Fill yourself up with so much good that there's no room for the bad.

*"Whatsoever things are true,
whatsoever things are honest,
whatsoever things are just,
whatsoever things are pure,
whatsoever things are lovely,
whatsoever things are of good report;
if there be any virtue,
and if there be any praise,
think on these things."*

Philippians 4:8

One of life's loveliest privileges is that
of teaching children the ways of Jesus,
in hopes that they may be spared
the consequences of sin
and one day enjoy the
thrill of eternity!

Training a child has to start on the inside –
with a loving relationship that protects
dignity and promotes respect.

Rules without relationship
breed rebellion.

$\mathcal{P}$ursuing the tasks that face us without fretting,
fussing or expressing
discontent is profitable,
for this is the work God has
given us to do.

It's whatever is "at hand."

As we complete the "at hand" things,
we find contentment and happiness.

𝒞herish happy times.
Use the memories to strengthen you
in times of sorrow or confusion.
Look ahead to pleasant possibilities of
more happy times yet to come.

Overcome your sorrow with joy!

A merry heart is good medicine,
not only for oneself, but for all those
whose lives touch ours.

Whenever one steps away from the crowd and sets out to do something that flows from a passion within, there will be onlookers who will murmur with criticism.

Assess your position. Make sure it is God leading you and then be obedient.

Press on past the doubting naysayers.

God will send people who understand and share your passion. They will come alongside to work with you as you take up your position.

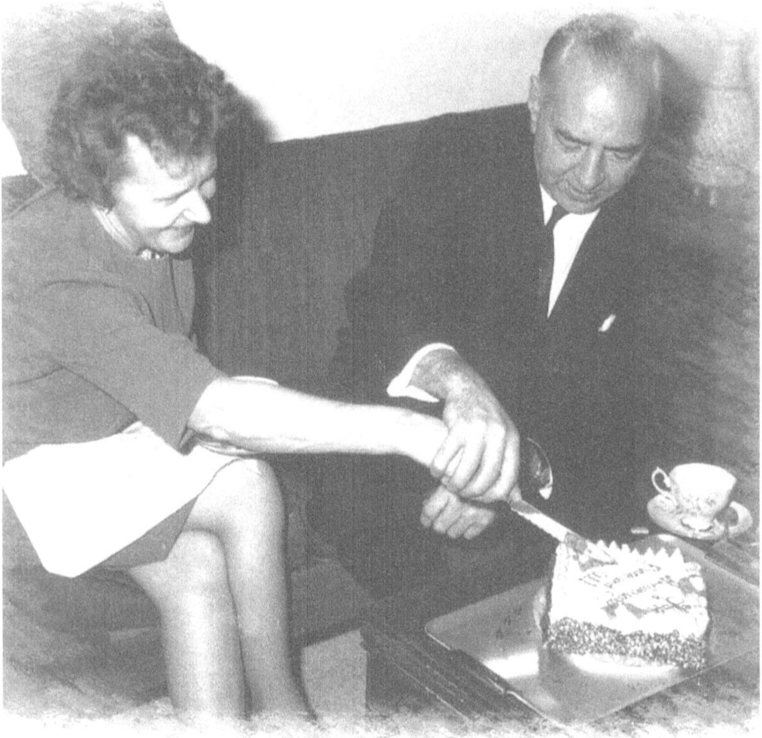

𝓕ear, confusion and pride block us
from the total surrender to God
that brings peace.

Letting go is the best way to hold on
—to God.

You know you've surrendered to God
when you stop manipulating circumstances
and trust that He is at work
on your behalf.

Money, power and fame are the prizes
sought by the people of the world.

But at the end of days, when one stands
before the Maker, will there be comfort where
there are no pedestals of privilege?

What happens to the wealthy when they
find themselves suddenly catapulted
into eternity with empty pockets
and no entourage; to the powerful when they stand
before the all-powerful God; to the famous where
only God is worthy of praise?

Where anyone will spend eternity depends on
whether the richness of their relationship with
Jesus exceeds the wealth in the bank accounts to
which they will no longer have access.

There is no one so miserable
as one who tries to live the Christian life
according to his or her own abilities.

When God looks at us, He sees us as though
totally covered by a blood red blanket
—the righteousness of Christ.

Not one inch of our humanity shows,
because not one inch of our humanity
could ever measure up.
It is the covering of the blood of Jesus
that gives us entrance to the courts of God.

It's not, "I believe in God, but I have this problem...."

Rather, "I have this problem, but I believe in God."

When one considers the tremendous
consequences that can come from
little things —
a word spoken,
a chance meeting
a tap on the shoulder,
the meeting of a gaze,
one wonders —
are there really any little things?

How sad it would be to get to the end
of one's life and still not be sure of the
purpose for living—particularly when it has been
right under our noses from
the beginning of life!

Every cell of nature in it's amazing design,
points us to relationship with our Maker,
the whole purpose for our being.

Milestones are good places for assessing where one is in light of the journey towards eternity.

Servants don't use their masters
for *their own* purposes.
They allow themselves to be used by their master
for *his* purposes.

For us to try to use God for our own
purposes is folly.

Wisdom is found in discovering
how He can use us.

𝒰se things,
never people.

It is a great disappointment
to receive attention only
when there is an ulterior motive.

In this world there are givers and there are takers.
Be known as a giver!

No one can feel happy all the time.
Despite our feelings,
we have an obligation to those around us
to be cheerful, interested in what
they are doing, and kind.

Because faith is the substance of things hoped for, yet unseen, we can *"call those things that are not as though they were."*
*R*omans 4:17

If we pray for something
we know to be within God's will,
we can expect His response
before we see any tangible evidence of it.

Pray with confidence.
It changes things.

If God permits a difficulty or trial
to come upon us, it must be because
it is the very best thing that could happen to us.

If a vase being shaped under the hands of a potter
could speak, it would complain of feeling totally
out of control spinning on the potter's wheel.
It would wince with the pain
of pressure exerted here and there.
It would complain of feeling like
nothing more than a lump of clay.

Only the Master Potter knows what He is doing as
He shapes us under the pressure of His hand.

When we look at life
from God's perspective,
we can give thanks in all circumstances.

*I*ndividuals who go through marriage
never looking at another person with
romantic interest are rare indeed.

How we get through those times of
testing determines
the happiness of later years.

At this stage of the game I can say with more confidence than ever, how important it is for young people to weather the storms and to stay true to their vows.

Holding fast to their faith until in later years one almost hears a cry of victory as the Glory of the setting sun softens and draws us together to realize what good companions we have become through the heat of the days' decisions and problems.

      Grace R.

Marriage is like a tea bag:
you don't know its strength
until it passes through hot water.

𝓕ifty-fifty relationships
don't usually last very long,
because people are always watching to make sure
they get their fifty percent.

Happy marriages happen
where each gives one-hundred percent.
Anything received back is a bonus.
Joy is the by-product of serving one another!

Better to hone skills of consideration and
brighten one's corner in the years of youth,
than find oneself old
and alone in the dark.

Of marriage, God says,
"The two shall become as one flesh."
*E*phesians 5:31

The process of *becoming* "one"
is progressive over the years,
as the two jostle back and forth,
finding where their strengths are appreciated
and their weaknesses need to be bolstered
by the strengths of the other.

Eventually, the two become recognized
as a smoothly oiled machine, each contributing
to the positive functioning of the unit.

They have *"become as one flesh."*

Fence-sitting Christians lead miserable lives,
unable to partake in either the rowdy
laughter of the unsaved
or the infectious joy of the redeemed.

Joy is buried deep in the heart of God.
To find it, one has to earnestly search
for God's heart and then enter in
and crawl down deep until totally
suffused by His love.

All sin starts in the mind as an evil thought.
If entertained and allowed to take root,
it will grow into an evil act.

How much more pleasant it is to keep one's mind
filled with lovely, healthy thoughts of kindness!

Thanking God for privileges,
instead of complaining about circumstances,
fills one's heart with
the peace of harmony with God.

Nothing in this life lasts forever—
those dearly loved, homes, cottages,
trinkets, positions, fame—
everything that surrounds us will one day be gone.

Only what's done for Christ will last.

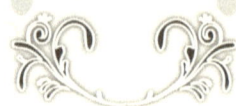

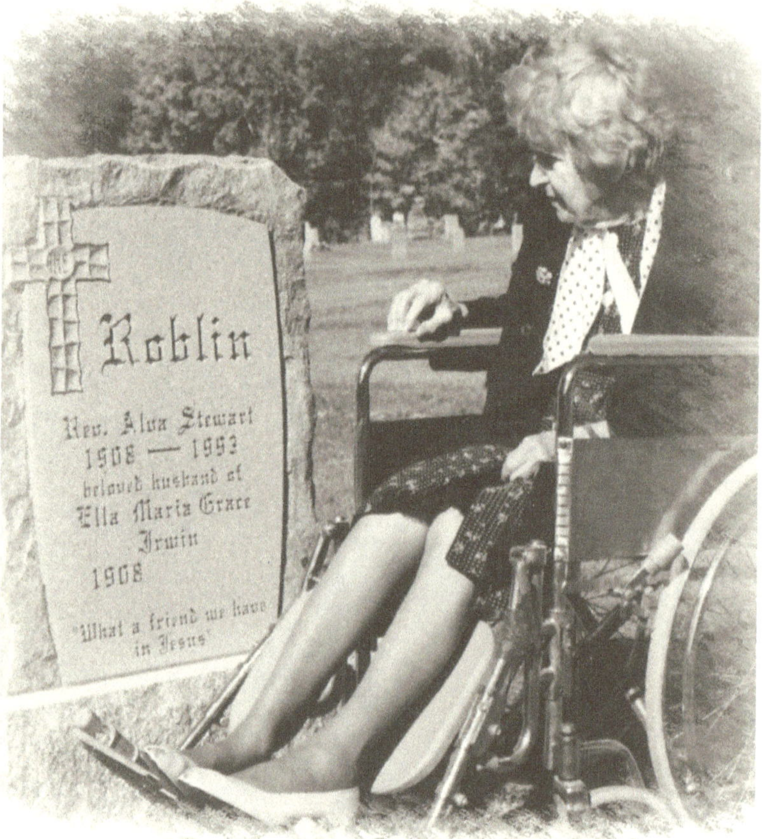
Roblin
Rev. Alva Stewart
1908 — 1993
beloved husband of
Ella Maria Grace
Irwin
1908
"What a friend we have
in Jesus"

There has been much debate
over heaven and hell;
whether they exist, where they are and
what sort of life one will live once there.

Skeptics say, "A God of love would never send people
to a place like hell," but they don't understand.
That's not His choice. It's ours.
He prepared heaven for us—but if we don't pay
attention to His directions for getting there,
we will be doomed to spend eternity
in the place He prepared for Satan.

People choose hell by default.
Choosing heaven is an active choice,
a benefit of choosing to believe in Jesus as God's Son
and committing one's life to Him.

Jesus *gave His life* to
keep people from hell.
But He prepared heaven for
those who love Him!

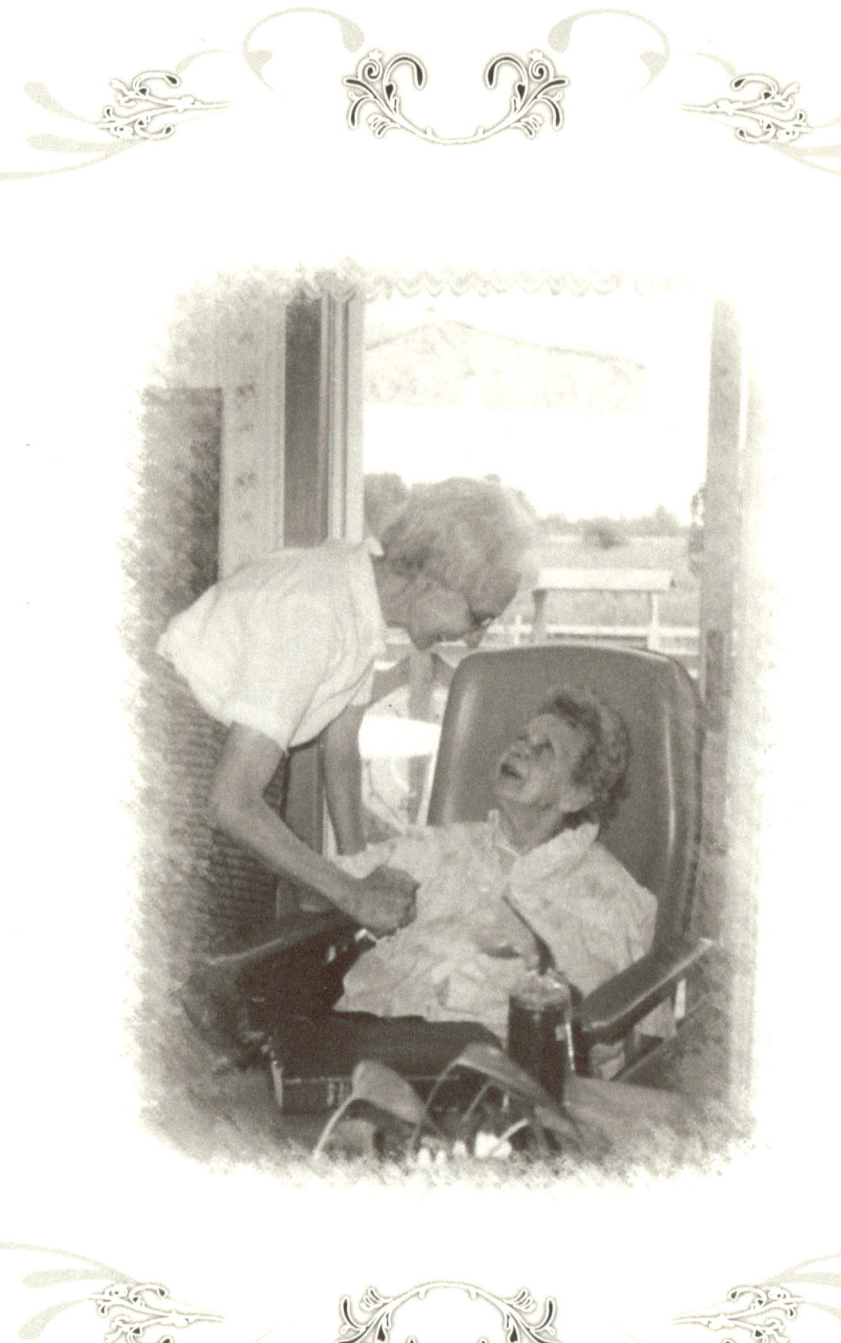

Aging is one of the most difficult
processes most people will ever
have to endure.

But it's not without purpose!

The job of caring for the elderly is designed to
increase compassion in the young,
to help them get their minds
off of themselves.

Priorities come into clearer focus with age.
The glitter of materialism and all the things for
which we strive in youth,
fade in light of the value of relationships.

The deterioration of one's body is a
sobering thing and leads those who have paid little
attention to God to examine their lives—
in light of preparation for eternity.

The work of the disabled and elderly can be the
most far-reaching and productive.

If one can do nothing but pray,
one can pray.

Prayer changes circumstances.
It has no boundaries.
It sets hosts of angels into action
on behalf of loved ones.
It is a direct link with the One
who knows our future.
It opens a dialogue of hope
where there would otherwise be none.
Prayer opens the windows of heaven,
allowing its comfort to rain down
on the lowly of heart.

With a dying breath, a lost soul may cry out to
God for forgiveness and enter
heaven, *"but only as one escaping
through the flames."*
1 Corinthians 3:15

How much better eternity will be if we can enter it
with truckloads of gifts for Jesus—
all the fruit of our service on earth,
treasure that will endure forever.

True sensitivity to the leading of God will come through a life devoted to prayer.

Grace reciting Psalm 139, her favorite,
at her 90th birthday party.

*"O Lord, you have searched me
and you know me.
You know when I sit and when I rise;
you perceive my thoughts from afar.
You discern my going out and my lying down;
you are familiar with all my ways.
Before a word is on my tongue
you know it completely, O Lord.
You hem me in —behind and before;
you have laid your hand upon me.
Such knowledge is too wonderful for me,
too lofty for me to attain.
Where can I go from your Spirit?
Where can I flee from your presence?
If I go up to the heavens, you are there;
if I make my bed in the depths, you are there.
If I rise on the wings of the dawn,
if I settle on the far side of the sea,
even there your hand will guide me,
your right hand will hold me fast."*

Psalm 139:1-10 (NIV)

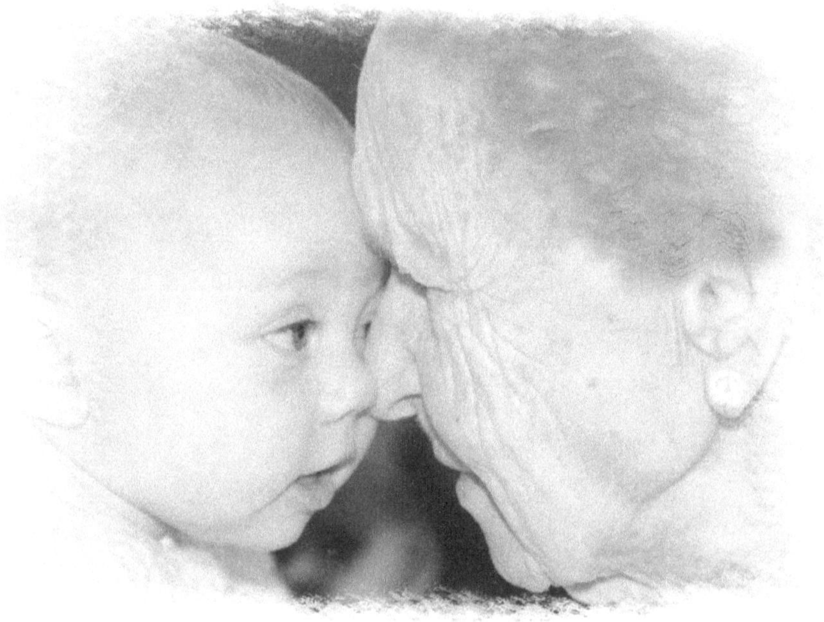

Physical birth brings physical life.
Spiritual birth (being born again)
brings spiritual life,
enabling one to dwell abundantly on earth
and eternally in heaven!

Mothers hold their children's hands for a little while—their hearts for a lifetime.

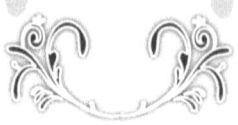

*I*n the instructions for her funeral, Grace Roblin wrote:

It is my earnest desire that there should be no lauditory discourse, eulogy or praise.

No statement or assurance that I should be worthy of Heavenly reward.

Rather may Christ be lifted up, that He may draw men and women to Himself.

Let my last wish be fulfilled, that Christ may be glorified, not I.

Forget the purpose for which friends have come together, and let the Spirit of God speak of important things.

Grace Roblin.

The Life of Grace

Because it was important to Grace that her life speak of Christ and not of herself, this book has focussed on the Christ-directed mind set that guided her life, rather than on the glorification of her as an individual.

Nevertheless, because some may be curious about her life, these few pages are dedicated to a brief history.

Born in 1908 on a farm, just outside Magnetawan, a tiny, northern Ontario town, Grace had two sisters; Jessie and Edith, and four brothers; Elmer, Will, Roy and Victor. Her parents, Georgeanna Stewart, a teacher, and Robert Irwin, a farmer, were second-generation Canadians of Irish and United Empire Loyalist stock.

The family lived a harsh, but bucolic life in a log cabin beside the Magnetawan River, until a two-story cedar-shake house was finally completed. It was little Grace's job to carry heavy pails of water up the hill from the river for the use of the family. Until the day she died, she was uncomfortable with the sound of tap water running unnecessarily.

At the tender age of four, little Grace was violated in the barn by a farmhand. The man ran off, never to be seen again, but the trauma left a deep scar on the child that manifested in later life as a painful shyness.

At the age of 11, in 1919, Grace and her older brother Will, walked two miles through the northern bush to a little Methodist church in Chapman Valley where an evangelist by the name of Elijah Brown was to be speaking. Reverend Brown spoke of sin and the human condition, of the need for repentance and salvation. With passion, he told of a spiritual birth, bringing new life through belief in the death and resurrection of Jesus Christ. All through the message, little Grace felt a great stirring in her heart. At the invitation to go to the front for prayer, both she and Will walked resolutely forward and committed their lives to Christ.

Halfway home, Grace sat on a rock in the middle of the forest. The sun filtered through the branches of the great northern pine trees as she gazed all around at the beauty of the woods. Never had the sky been bluer, the air been fresher nor the grass greener. She was now fully alive and equipped to fulfill her purpose in life.

Putting her love for music to work, Grace became the organist of the Magnetawan United Church at the age of 14 and fully involved herself in the church youth group.

After completion of high school in North Bay, she continued her studies in voice and nursing in Ann Arbor, Michigan. With the death of her father when she was 18, Grace returned to Ontario and moved to Toronto as companion and secretary to a wonderful old gentleman, Dr. Powell, who always summered at his cottage near Magnetawan.

While in Toronto, Grace attended Toronto Bible College and was swept off her feet by a handsome theological student, Al Roblin. Galloping his horse, Bubbles, through the Don Valley ravine to the elegant

Rosedale home of Dr. Powell, Al courted Grace with all the romance that could fill a girl's dreams. Two years later, in 1933, they were wed under a cedar arch in Magnetawan.

Ministering in Manilla, Ontario in 1935, Al built a idyllic little fish pond and a seat around a tree to welcome Grace and baby Dona Dee home from the hospital. Despite the fact that more of their earnings came from the gardens and smokehouses of the congregation than in monetary form, their home was always open to the community. Big pots of hot chocolate always simmered on Grace's stove for noisy young people gathering after skating parties on nearby ponds.

Seniors today, who were once part of the youth group, remember the influence Al and Grace had on their young lives. They remember Grace's blonde hair tucked neatly into a bun at the nape of her neck and her warm hospitality. With smiles, they remember Al's fun-loving exuberance for life, his high spirits and wonderful enthusiasm for the Gospel message. In the fall, when Al enrolled at McMaster University, he and Grace moved their ministry to Mountsberg, closer to classes in Hamilton.

In 1938, the Baptist Home Mission Board arranged for Al to minister in Slate River, a mission outpost near Thunder Bay, Ontario. The magnitude of the need for the Gospel in the northern areas was great. Living in the parsonage attached to the little white church, the young couple talked long into the nights about how to reach the remote areas with the love of God.

It was the "Dirty Thirties." Ministry meant feeding and clothing the needy with relief boxes. With a mixture of German, Swedish, Norwegian and Finnish immigrants waging a desperate struggle to gain a foothold on strip farms, language barriers added to the complexities of ministering to the needs of the community.

Grace organized a "Dorcas Society" for young women to study the Gospel and sew and distribute clothing to those in need in remote areas. For the children, she coordinated the first Daily Vacation Bible School with stories, games, crafts and snacks. It became her pattern for every summer thereafter, until she was well into her eighties.

Al pioneered the first Gospel radio work in the area, once skiing 17 miles through six feet of loose snow, through a dark and dangerous $30^0\,F$ night to Fort William to host his morning radio broadcast. Knowing Al was about his Master's business, Grace never objected to his admittedly adventurous exploits.

They opened several schoolhouses for ministry in frontier outstations. With the acquisition of a panel truck to pick up children from the remote farms, Al and Grace developed a far-reaching Sunday School program that enabled them to communicate the love of Jesus in a tangible way.

It was during those years that Al's compassion became unglued from his reserve and he fathered his only son with a troubled woman. With great anguish of heart, life went on.

Rather than expose her husband's sin and destroy their ability to spread the message of Christ, Grace chose to forgive Al and let the Lord work through the circumstances. In all those years, she confided in no one but God and sought the advice of no man or woman. Her trust was in God alone. She was determined not to allow human weakness to short-circuit God's call on their lives. She knew they had a job to do and she knew that by applying the message of the Gospel to her responses to the challenges of life, they could experience the overcoming power of God.

Some may ask why, when Grace so graciously rose above the situation, this should now be told.

The reason is this: Grace's strength and godliness resulted in fifty years of wonderful ministry that would otherwise have been thwarted. Many lives were changed for the better. Many received eternal life who would otherwise have perished. Al did not escape unscathed, but suffered lifelong bouts of depression, longing to be a father to his only son. In the spiritual realm, his sin was forgiven through deep repentance. Now, Al and Grace have both gone home to Glory and the testimony of God's ability to mend broken hearts, despite man's weakness, gives greater glory to Him than silence could ever afford.

It is important for young couples to know that they may suffer great pain in their relationships, but the answers do not lie in self-righteous self-justification or hours of dirt-dredging counselling. The answers lie in holding fast to the promises of God, in putting His Word to practical work in one's life.

In no way did Grace take it upon herself to make her husband pay for his sin. She simply loved him, cared for him and let God look after the rest. Consequently, her daughters never needed to go through the devastation of divorce and she and her husband were able to fulfill God's calling on their lives. When, in 2001, the girls discovered they had a brother, they experienced deeper understanding of the grace of God. The message of the Gospel became even more relevant in their lives. The son, a wonderful man with many of his father's giftings, was finally able to settle into being himself.

In 1940, Al returned to McMaster to complete his degree. Appreciative of Grace's love for the Lord and her passion for the furtherance of the Gospel, the Slate River deacons recognized her unnatural wisdom and asked her to carry on the work of the church until Al's return.

Refusing to acknowledge the shyness that dogged her and threatened to thwart her leadership abilities, Grace took up her pastoral duties by focussing on her confidence in God and the needs around her. Travelling 25 miles with little Dona Dee, back and forth over terribly rutted roads to the various outposts she and Al had established, she preached, visited the ill, conducted Sunday Schools, held prayer meetings and hosted the radio program. Dependent on an old, unreliable Chevy, she became creative in dealing with mechanical problems. Once, when out in the middle of nowhere with little Dona Dee by her side, Grace discovered a hole in her gas tank. "Here," she said, handing a piece of gum to her daughter, "chew this, sweetheart." Once softened, the gum was 'grace-fully' affixed to the offending hole and off they went!

Al's return to Slate River, following his graduation, was of short duration. With World War II having broken out in 1939, he felt the call to chaplaincy services and was subsequently sent to Air Force Command Headquarters in Montreal. Much loved by the Slate River people, Grace resumed her duties until another minister could be found and she was able to join Al in Montreal.

With thousands of men gone, the women of Canada were called on to keep the country going. Both St. Paul's and Rosemount Baptist Churches in Montreal were without pastors. Knowing of her move to Montreal, the Baptist administration asked Grace to fill the vacancies. With total reliance on God, Grace complied.

Barely settling in to their new routines, the family was once again separated. The Air Force dispatched Al to Victoriaville, then to Coal Harbor on North Vancouver Island and on to Edmonton, where he became Command Chaplain of the Northwest Air Command Staging Route.

Alone in Montreal, Grace and Dona Dee, now eight, tried to make the best of things. It was the era of the "Zoot Suiters," roving bands of thugs wearing long, wide-lapelled jackets with baggy, tight-cuffed pants and wide-brimmed fedoras, their badges of delinquency. Despite the nine o'clock citywide curfew, they prowled the streets at night, precipitating headlines of assaults and murders. Resolutely, Grace determined to minister the message of the Gospel. Whispering a prayer for safety for little Dona Dee as she left her in the locked apartment while she went to conduct the services, Grace routinely walked down the middle of the dark, Montreal streets to avoid attack from Zoot Suiters lurking in the shadows. God was faithful. In conversations with Dona in later years, she was never afraid when left alone and simply accepted the circumstances as a matter of course.

In the fall of 1944, at Grace's request, the Montreal churches were able to replace her, so that she and Dona Dee could join Al in Edmonton. When they arrived, Al had a lovely, two-bedroom apartment waiting. The master bedroom was a very large room with a big window and elegant draperies. The other, much smaller bedroom with cozy, kitten wallpaper and a single bed, was perfect for a little girl. Assuming that Dona Dee would be thrilled with the kittens, Al smiled and said, "You can choose whichever room you want, sweetheart."

Without a blink, Dona pointed in the direction of the master bedroom and said, "I want that one!"

And so it was that Grace and Al's reunion was slightly cramped in a single bed with playful kittens on the walls. Nine months later, Al having been transferred overseas in February as Leader of the Bison Squadron and Grace having returned to Ontario to her brother's family on an Uxbridge farm, Diane Elaine arrived in a world of uncertainty.

Blue airmail letters, eagerly awaited on both sides of the ocean, were the only tangible consolation for families separated by war. So precious, they were treasured in mounting stacks and seldom discarded, even after victory was declared.

Once able to travel after the birth of the baby, Grace took Dona and Diane to her brother Roy's family in Mindemoya, on the Manitoulin Island, where she was offered a home until Al returned just after Diane's first birthday.

By the time Al and Grace were able to establish a home together again, it was 1947. They were called to Silverthorne Baptist Church in northwest Toronto. With Grace's mother having gone blind, they added her to the household until her death in 1951. No matter where Grace went, she found particular areas of need and enjoyed working with the church people organizing groups to satisfy those needs. At Silverthorne, there was particular need for a mothers' group. Once up and running, it flourished, as did the children's Daily Vacation Bible School, which Grace conducted every summer in the month of July.

With a high level of crime in the area, including several thefts from the church, Al set a trap for the ruffians and caught three gang-members breaking into the church one night. Chasing them through the church yard and over a fence, he caught one by the shirt-tail and subdued him. From that initial contact, Al gradually met the other gang-members and organized them into a hockey league. Their opportunity to participate was dependant on their attendance in Sunday School, church and the youth group. Thus it was that Grace opened their home to the delinquents of the area for dynamic youth meetings. Many had life-changing experiences and several of those boys went on in their faith into the ministry.

For five happy years, the family stabilized in the beautiful new house Al had built with his military earnings. Nevertheless, when the call came to serve in ministry at Park Street Baptist in Peterborough, sentiment dissolved in face of obedience to God's call. Grace packed up the family's belongings and left her beautiful leaded glass windows and stone fireplaces, built, stone by stone, by Al—for a big old parsonage.

In Peterborough, Grace soon recognized the need for seniors' ministry and initiated the "Over Seventy Group," where members shared Christian experiences, used their talents and enjoyed afternoon tea. Once again, children's work was a priority. Feeling the need to expand Vacation School opportunities, Grace held after-school Bible Clubs in her home, where children would drop in for flannel-graph stories and cookies. Many accepted Jesus into their lives and kept in touch with Grace through the years.

Ever conscious of Biblical directives, Grace honored Sundays as holy days, even though they were not technically "Sabbath" days. There was no confusing a Sunday with any other day. Saturdays were "preparation" days, when anything needed for Sundays was purchased, shoes were shined, silver was polished and bottom chair rungs were dusted. In answer to Diane's occasional suggestion that no one would notice if the bottom rungs were dusted, the smiling reply was always the same: "Maybe not, but they'll notice if they're not!"

It was not unusual for young couples to make appointments to seek Grace's wisdom concerning a variety of topics. More than one couple struggling with infertility welcomed a healthy baby into their home after prayer with her.

While in Peterborough, Al secured a cottage on Lake Mississauga, a half-hour's drive from the city. There the family spent the month of August and occasional holidays each year. In the woodlands, Grace's love for work translated into raking twigs and dead leaves into great piles at the edge of the lake for evening bonfires, around which friends and family would gather for happy times of chatter and singing. Church members were as welcome at the cottage as they were in the church pews. To Grace, ministry was a welcome part of the fabric of life and knew no holidays or boundaries. Both she and Al were always delighted to see cars of friends and family approaching over the rough cottage roads.

To minister to the cottagers, they organized Sunday services, conducted with a microphone, from the balcony of a boathouse. It was on an island, close enough to the mainland, that a rope where boats could be tied, was stretched across the water. The occupants simply stayed in their boats and enjoyed the services with ripplets of waves gently lapping against their hulls.

From Peterborough, in 1956, Al was called back into the Air Force for a year of special duty in Winnipeg. In response to the question of housing, he purchased a 37-foot mobile home in which Grace and 11-year-old Diane would live in Winnipeg while he travelled back and forth from there to Cold Lake, Alberta. By this time, Dona had graduated and was teaching school in Ontario. Ever diligent in seeking opportunities to serve God wherever she was, Grace not only served as Devotional Convener for the Military Women's Guild, but secured permission and space from the Winnipeg Air Force Base to organize a Daily Vacation Bible School for the children of the military. After planning for 60 children and organizing adequate staff, Grace was pleasantly surprised when 137 children registered. The Commanding Officer of the Base was so pleased with the results that he thanked Grace and promised to make sure that there would be another school for the children the following year when she would be gone.

Lonely evenings without Al were never empty. She kept herself occupied filling whatever needs presented themselves, whether tending a fussy baby for a harried neighbor or writing words of encouragement to some troubled soul or misguided politician. It was not unusual for Diane to wake up in the morning with a new outfit Grace had sewn in the wee hours, hanging on her doorknob to be worn to school that morning.

From 1955 to 1963 at First Baptist in Sudbury and then until 1968 at Weston Baptist in Toronto, Grace's main focus was, once again, children's work, although she also worked extensively in women's programs that were already well underway when she arrived. Whether carrying on from someone else's initiative or finding ways to minister in areas of need, her diligence was the same.

In Sudbury, opportunity opened up, not only for another radio program, but for helping to pioneer Canadian television ministry. The radio program, "Songs by Candlelight," was a warm presentation of Christian music recordings interspersed with gentle thoughts. The television program featured Al speaking, Grace and Diane telling stories to groups of children, and the singing of area Christians.

While still in Sudbury, then Prime Minister Diefenbaker and his wife Olive were scheduled to visit the city and dedicate the "Big Nickel." Since they were Baptists, Al received notification that they would be attending his church on Sunday morning. Reasoning that they would have to have lunch somewhere, he wrote to the Prime Minister's office and invited the Diefenbakers to lunch. When the day came, following the service, Al, Grace, Diane and their other guests led the way, followed by the Prime Minister's car and an extensive motorcade. Grace served pork tenderloin shish kebobs with rice, salad and vegetables, followed by one of her fabulous desserts. The house shone, but not any more than it would have for anyone else visiting. The food was exquisitely prepared, but not any more exquisitely than it would have been for anyone else. The conversation sparkled, but not any moreso than it would have with other guests sitting at her table. Grace's journal entry for May 16, 1965, read, *"Mr. and Mrs. Diefenbaker and Dr. Cooke,*

Brian, Barry, Diane, Dad and I here for dinner. Diane and Barry left for Toronto at 3 p.m. S.S. teachers meeting." From where Grace lived, at the foot of the cross, no man stood higher than any other. The ground was level.

From Sudbury, Diane left for Acadia University and began fifteen years of rebellion from the faith. Grace was deeply saddened to see her youngest daughter take a path that would surely lead to difficulties. She waited and prayed, knowing the rebel would one day open her eyes—which she did, but not without much fasting and agreement in prayer between Grace and her sister, Jessie Hogan. Upon her return, Diane had a very deep appreciation for the work of Jesus in her life, but the fruit of her rebellion led to many challenges in her life.

At Mount Calvary, in Hamilton, where Al and Grace ministered from 1968 to 1973, Grace started three youth groups for different ages and a Tuesday night group, "The Learn and Live Club," in which all ages participated with gusto. No matter what she started at any church, Grace built the foundations strong, training others to seamlessly continue the work when she was gone.

Here and there throughout the years, she wrote articles on Christian living, conducted workshops and took leadership in missions work. Music was always a big part of her life. Wherever her services were required in playing the organ, leading the choir or singing solos, she filled the need.

In 1973, at the age of 65, Al and Grace moved to Bobcaygeon and took a retirement pastoate in Fenelon Falls. Recognizing a great need for ministry to the elderly and shut-ins of the area, Grace organized and coordinated a "Meals on Wheels" program and, true to pattern, conducted a Daily Vacation Bible School in Fenelon for over fifteen years.

With Al's diagnosis of Alzheimer's in 1992, he and Grace sold their home and moved into an apartment built for them at Diane's in Argyle, an hour and a half north-east of Toronto. After 60 years in ministry, they celebrated their 60th wedding anniversary in 1993, just seven months prior to Al's death from Alzheimer's and heart failure.

Grace continued to live on with Diane and her family until her death in March of 2005, with a five-year interval in a nursing home.

Upon her death at age 96, at home with Diane, as Diane sang to her, Grace suddenly saw her brother, Victor, who had passed on several years before, but who was sent to escort his sister to the pearly gates. Greeting him with great joy in her voice, she took his hand and passed from earth to eternity.

At the celebration of her life in March of 2006, the church was filled with people whose lives had been made better by knowing her.

At the bottom of a page recording her activities over the years, Grace had written, *"Through Christ I have done that which I could not do."*

"*Your Word, O Lord, is eternal; it stands firm in the heavens. Your faithfulness continues through all generations...*"

Psalm 119:89,90 (NIV)

Great-grandchildren.

www.ingramcontent.com/pod-product-compliance
Lightning Source LLC
Chambersburg PA
CBHW030104240426
43661CB00001B/11